Travel To... COOLEST COLLECTIONS

Kaitlyn Duling

Rourke Educational Media

A Division of Carson Dellosa Education

ROURKE'S SCHOOL to HOME CONNECTIONS
BEFORE AND DURING READING ACTIVITIES

Before Reading: *Building Background Knowledge and Vocabulary*

Building background knowledge can help children process new information and build upon what they already know. Before reading a book, it is important to tap into what children already know about the topic. This will help them develop their vocabulary and increase their reading comprehension.

Questions and Activities to Build Background Knowledge:

1. Look at the front cover of the book and read the title. What do you think this book will be about?
2. What do you already know about this topic?
3. Take a book walk and skim the pages. Look at the table of contents, photographs, captions, and bold words. Did these text features give you any information or predictions about what you will read in this book?

Vocabulary: *Vocabulary Is Key to Reading Comprehension*

Use the following directions to prompt a conversation about each word.

- Read the vocabulary words.
- What comes to mind when you see each word?
- What do you think each word means?

Vocabulary Words:
- antiquities
- artifacts
- bicultural
- colonized
- conserved
- curator
- deaccessions
- exhibition
- Indigenous
- preservation
- repatriation
- restored

During Reading: *Reading for Meaning and Understanding*

To achieve deep comprehension of a book, children are encouraged to use close reading strategies. During reading, it is important to have children stop and make connections. These connections result in deeper analysis and understanding of a book.

 ### Close Reading a Text

During reading, have children stop and talk about the following:

- Any confusing parts
- Any unknown words
- Text to text, text to self, text to world connections
- The main idea in each chapter or heading

Encourage children to use context clues to determine the meaning of any unknown words. These strategies will help children learn to analyze the text more thoroughly as they read.

When you are finished reading this book, turn to page 46 for **Text-Dependent Questions** an an **Extension Activity**.

TABLE of CONTENTS

Massive Museums and Landmark Collections 4

You Collect *What?* 12

Preserving Culture and Community 22

Creepy (and Crawly!) Collections 30

Interacting with Art 38

We Traveled to 44

Glossary 45

Index 46

Text-Dependent Questions 46

Extension Activity 46

Bibliography 47

About the Author 48

MASSIVE MUSEUMS
AND LANDMARK COLLECTIONS

Coins. Sneakers. Stamps. T-shirts. People of all ages have fun collecting objects, from special souvenirs to random gadgets. The collections might look different, but they all hold meaning. The objects are important to the person or group that collects and organizes them.

Museums and other public collections aren't so different. They are just like personal collections of stuffed animals and homemade art…but many are on a massive scale! Across the globe, there are more than 95,000 museums, each with their own collections of objects that are organized, exhibited, and **conserved** so that they may be enjoyed for years to come. Collections help us learn about different cultures, preserve the past, and think about what we want the future to look like.

The National Museum of Natural History in Paris, France

THE LOUVRE

PARIS, FRANCE

The Galerie d'Apollon (Apollo Gallery) in the Louvre

Mona Lisa by Leonardo da Vinci

The Louvre

Today, museums old and new have expanded to include more objects and bigger buildings. The Louvre in Paris, France, is the largest museum in the world. As you walk through its art galleries, you can explore almost 10,000 years of history! The museum has around 480,000 works of art recorded in their digital collection, but that is only about three-quarters of what they own in all. On display, there are 35,000 works of art at a time. Just to see each piece of art on display it would take you about 200 days. That might earn the award for longest field trip ever!

LET'S GET DIGITAL

When disaster strikes or global pandemic looms, popular museums can empty out in an instant. That's why many of today's most popular collections are going through a digitization process. Online exhibits open up the possibility of "virtual visits" to museums. That way, no matter where you live or what your life looks like, you can easily explore world-class collections. You can make a virtual visit to the Louvre right now!

THE BRITISH MUSEUM
LONDON, ENGLAND

Museum collections with extensive galleries of objects representing millions of years of history, art, and culture, can come together in curious ways. Some of their objects are donated. Others are purchased. In some of the world's oldest museums, objects have been acquired through less respectable means. Some items have been looted and then stolen or sold. You can find **artifacts** from countries that were **colonized** in history museums on the other side of the planet!

This moai statue can be found in the British Museum but is originally from Rapa Nui (Easter Island).

The British Museum

The British Museum in London, England, is known as the first public national museum on Earth. But not all of its objects came from the island of Great Britain. In fact, after it was established in 1753, the museum began amassing a collection of objects from around the world because of the reach of the British Empire. Some might even say these objects were *stolen*. The British Empire was made up of Great Britain and its colonies. The colonies were countries that Great Britain settled into and established control over for their own use. Look closely at the galleries, and you can follow the trail paved by the Empire. **Antiquities** from ancient Greece, Egypt, Sudan, Canada, and countless other nations are part of the British Museum's permanent collection.

GAME ON

The British Museum holds 82 of the Lewis Chessmen, a group of chess pieces carved from walrus ivory in the 12th century. The medieval pieces, which were discovered near Lewis Island in Scotland, are known as the most famous chess pieces in the world! Eleven of these priceless pieces are housed at the National Museum of Scotland.

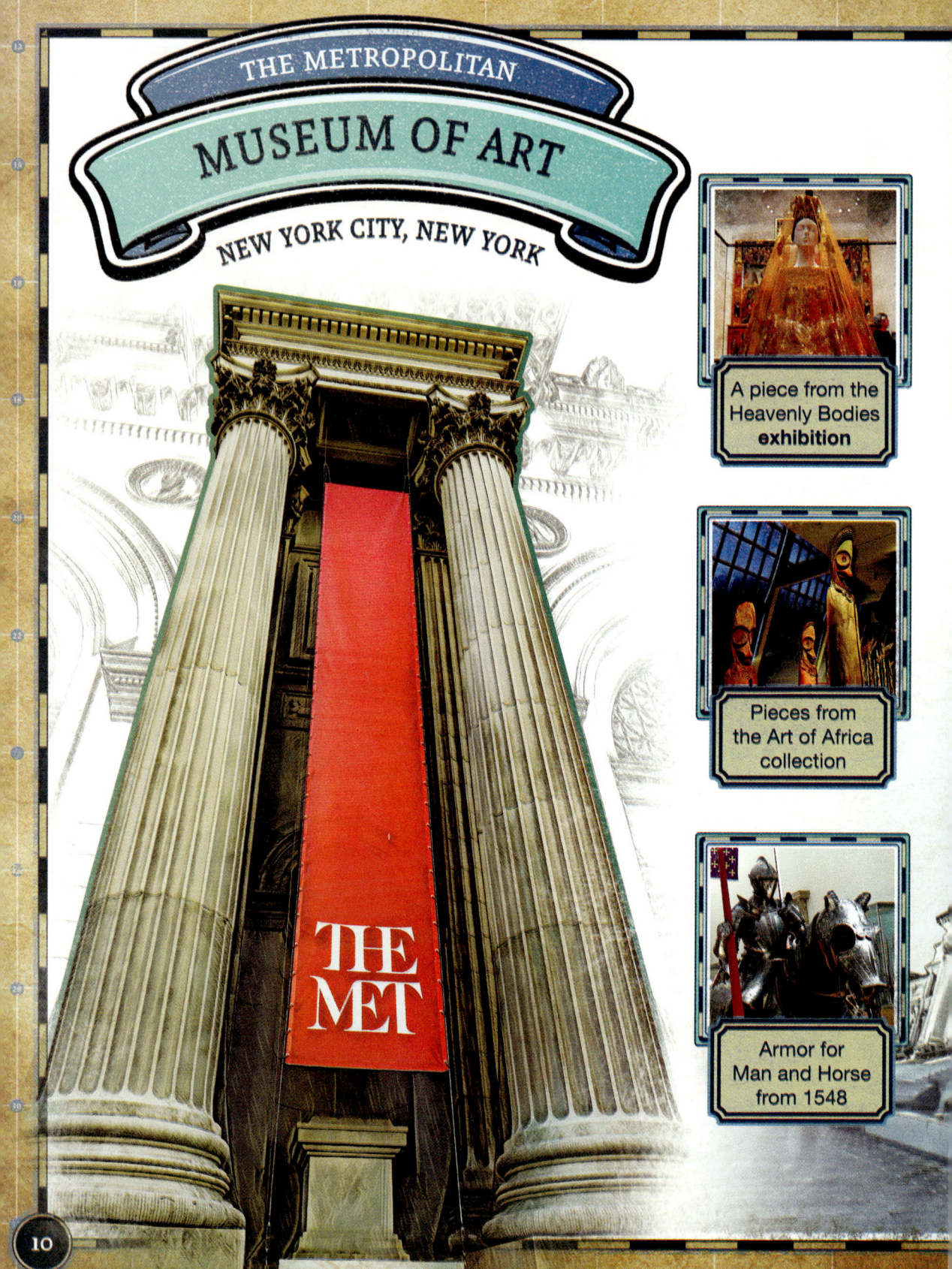

Museum collections are always growing. The Metropolitan Museum of Art (the Met) in New York City is the largest art museum in the United States and is still growing! The Met is constantly acquiring new paintings, sculptures, and more. In 2020, the museum accepted over 2,500 new works! But the building can only hold so many works, so the museum also sells, or **deaccessions**, art each year.

The Met

DEACCESSIONING IN HARD TIMES

During the COVID-19 pandemic, museums across the globe had to close. Some turned to deaccessioning to stay afloat. This controversial practice is surprisingly common. What do you think? Would you ever sell an item from your most prized collection?

YOU COLLECT WHAT?

What do lunch boxes, neon lights, toilets, hair, and burnt food have in common? They all have museums dedicated to them! That's right—collections come in all shapes and sizes, and can hold everything from ancient objects to fresh fruits. That's not an exaggeration. Fuefukigawa Fruit Park in Yamanashi, Japan, is home to a fruit-themed greenhouse, theater, restaurant, and museum. Visitors flock to the glass-domed museum to learn about the history and beauty of fruit.

The Fruit Museum of Fuefukigawa is just one sweet example of the many unique museums that focus on singular objects or themes. The British Lawnmower Museum in northern England celebrates everyone's favorite piece of garden machinery; the Lunch Box Museum in Columbus, Georgia, is home to thousands of lunch boxes, all organized alphabetically by the character on the front of the box; and Leila's Hair Museum in Independence, Missouri, displays antique human hair that has been turned into wreaths, jewelry, and other "hair objects." If an object exists, chances are, someone collects it.

THE NATIONAL MUSTARD MUSEUM
MIDDLETON, WISCONSIN

When it comes to collections, one of the most pressing concerns is **preservation**. Museum staff members work tirelessly to preserve and protect valuable artworks, statues, and more. In the world of food museums, that challenge is extra difficult…and sometimes delicious! The National Mustard Museum in Middleton, Wisconsin, can't promise that any of the over 6,000 mustards on display are fresh, but they sure are interesting!

Museum founder and **curator** Barry Levenson started collecting mustards in the 1980s. Levenson was a lawyer, and one day, while he was arguing a case before the Supreme Court, he carried a tiny jar of mustard in his pocket. He won the case! Now mustard fans travel from all over the U.S. to see the impressive collection Levenson cooked up in Wisconsin.

**YELLOW
DIJON
GREY-POUPON
SPICY BROWN
GERMAN**

Natural MUSTARD MILD

**FRENCH
HONEY
WHOLE GRAIN
HOT
CREOLE**

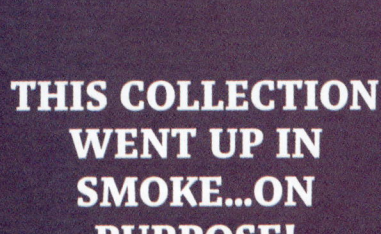

THIS COLLECTION WENT UP IN SMOKE…ON PURPOSE!

The Burnt Food Museum in Arlington, Massachusetts, serves up displays of spectacularly overcooked food. Some of the food is so horribly singed, you might mistake the exhibit for a fossil display. How do they keep the foods preserved for years without disintegrating? Now that's the chef's secret.

THE MUSEUM OF BREAD CULTURE
ULM, GERMANY

A display showing the inflated price of bread in the 1920s

The Museum of Bread Culture

Hungry for a sandwich to pair with those thousands of mustards? Look no further than one not-so-crusty collection: The Museum of Bread Culture in Ulm, Germany. This rural museum, which is housed in an old storehouse, tells the story of breadmaking, from human's first dabbles in dough to today's pre-sliced creations, tracing a 6,000-year history.

Willy Eiselen and his son Hermann began their bread collection in 1955, and it has since grown to include over 16,000 artifacts, from breadmaking equipment and cookbooks to paintings featuring bread and miniature kitchens. At the museum, guests can even try grinding grain the old-fashioned way—by hand. Remember: This collection should always be viewed on a full stomach. Otherwise, you're bound to get hungry halfway through!

A replica of an early 20th-century bakery inside the museum

The Sulabh International Museum of Toilets
Delhi, India

You may want to sit down when you see our next stop on this road trip through curious collections. The Sulabh International Museum of Toilets in Delhi, India, is dedicated to the history of toilets and health. Its collection includes everything from ornately decorated chamber pots and painted privies to modern bidets and mobile commodes. For those who just can't get enough toilet talk, the museum also has a collection of toilet-related poems.

1920s model of a two-story wooden outhouse

A leather chair toilet used by European nobility

The collection is organized chronologically, from oldest to newest. Visitors start by learning about toilets from the third millennium BCE and end their tour with the latest and greatest toilet models. Visitors can see a tabletop toilet from medieval England, as well as high-tech toilets from Japan.

A Chinese toilet bucket

MEET THE COLLECTOR

The Sulabh International Museum of Toilets was founded by Dr. Bindeshwar Pathak, a sociologist and social reformer. Dr. Pathak sees his collection as more than a museum. He is committed to the movements for environmental sanitation, waste management, and human rights.

THE NEON MUSEUM
LAS VEGAS, NEVADA

In Las Vegas, Nevada, one museum collection is lighting up the Strip. Las Vegas has long been known for its brightly colored neon signs. The Neon Museum is dedicated to telling the story of Las Vegas through its massive collection of signs, which includes **restored** and unrestored pieces from the 1930s through today.

Visitors don't just come to the Neon Museum to learn about neon signs. Many consider it the perfect backdrop for wedding photos, engagements, family portraits, and social media snapshots. As social media expands and camera technology improves, more and more museums are taking a photo-friendly approach.

The Neon Museum

The Neon Boneyard

PRESERVING CULTURE AND COMMUNITY

THE NATIONAL MUSEUM OF AFRICAN AMERICAN HISTORY AND CULTURE
WASHINGTON, D.C.

Museum collections don't just display art and other objects. They tell important stories from the past, ground us in the present, and help us to imagine the future.

Have you ever visited a cultural museum? The Smithsonian National Museum of African American History and Culture (NMAAHC) in Washington, D.C., was created to document the past, present, and future of African American life, history, and culture. NMAAHC opened in 2016, but the push to create such a museum began in 1915, when Black veterans of the Civil War started the conversation and began to raise money for a monument on the National Mall.

Today, the NMAAHC's incredible collection includes more than 36,000 objects, including Harriet Tubman's hymnal, Hank Aaron's baseball jersey, a plane flown by the Tuskegee Airmen, and even a plantation cabin.

The NMAAHC

The NMAAHC holds events where they collaborate with other museums, educational institutions, and people who are also working to preserve and explore African American history.

THE MUSEUM OF NEW ZEALAND
TE PAPA TONGAREWA
WELLINGTON, NEW ZEALAND

Cultural museums help preserve the past, oftentimes for groups of people who have been marginalized, displaced, or discriminated against. These museums help ensure that no people's history will ever be completely erased. The Museum of New Zealand Te Papa Tongarewa (Te Papa), which translates to "our container of treasured things and people that spring from Mother Earth here in New Zealand," focuses on preserving cultural treasures of both the **Indigenous** Maori people and those who arrived when the land was colonized.

New Zealand, which was annexed by Holland in the 1600s and colonized by Britain in the 1800s, has a complicated national identity. Through its collections and programs, Te Papa hopes to tell that complex story and create a **bicultural** partnership between New Zealanders and Indigenous peoples.

Te Papa works to recover ancestral remains of Maori people from around the world.

Te Papa

THE EGYPTIAN MUSEUM
CAIRO, EGYPT

Today, some museums are working on **repatriation**. This is the process by which cultural objects are returned to their home countries.

In recent years, Egypt has stepped up efforts to recover stolen and smuggled antiquities. Visit museums in the United States, Britain, and across the world, and you are likely to see Egyptian **artifacts**, such as coffins and documents, that were once looted from Egypt. The Egyptian Museum is a museum that has its own collection of Egyptian artifacts—right in Cairo, Egypt. The collection of more than 120,000 items represents over 5,000 years of Egyptian history. As more objects are recovered, the collection will continue to grow.

The Egyptian Museum

King Tutankhamun's death mask

ANCIENT TREASURES

The Rosetta Stone is an ancient slab that helped experts unlock the secrets to Egyptian hieroglyphs. British soldiers captured the stone in 1801 and donated it to the British Museum in London, England. The priceless stone remains at the top of many wish lists of objects that could one day be repatriated and returned home to Egypt.

THE MUSEUM OF BLACK CIVILIZATIONS
DAKAR, SENEGAL

In 2018, a sprawling, new museum opened in Dakar, Senegal. The Museum of Black Civilizations tells the stories of Africa and Black civilizations across the globe. The staff members hope to reclaim African art and cultural objects that were stolen during colonial periods, and the circular building has room for around 18,000 pieces of art. However, many of the galleries are currently empty. In time, the museum's collection will grow, and visitors will be able to explore African art right where it was created— in Africa.

Cedar Men by Jems Robert Koko Bi

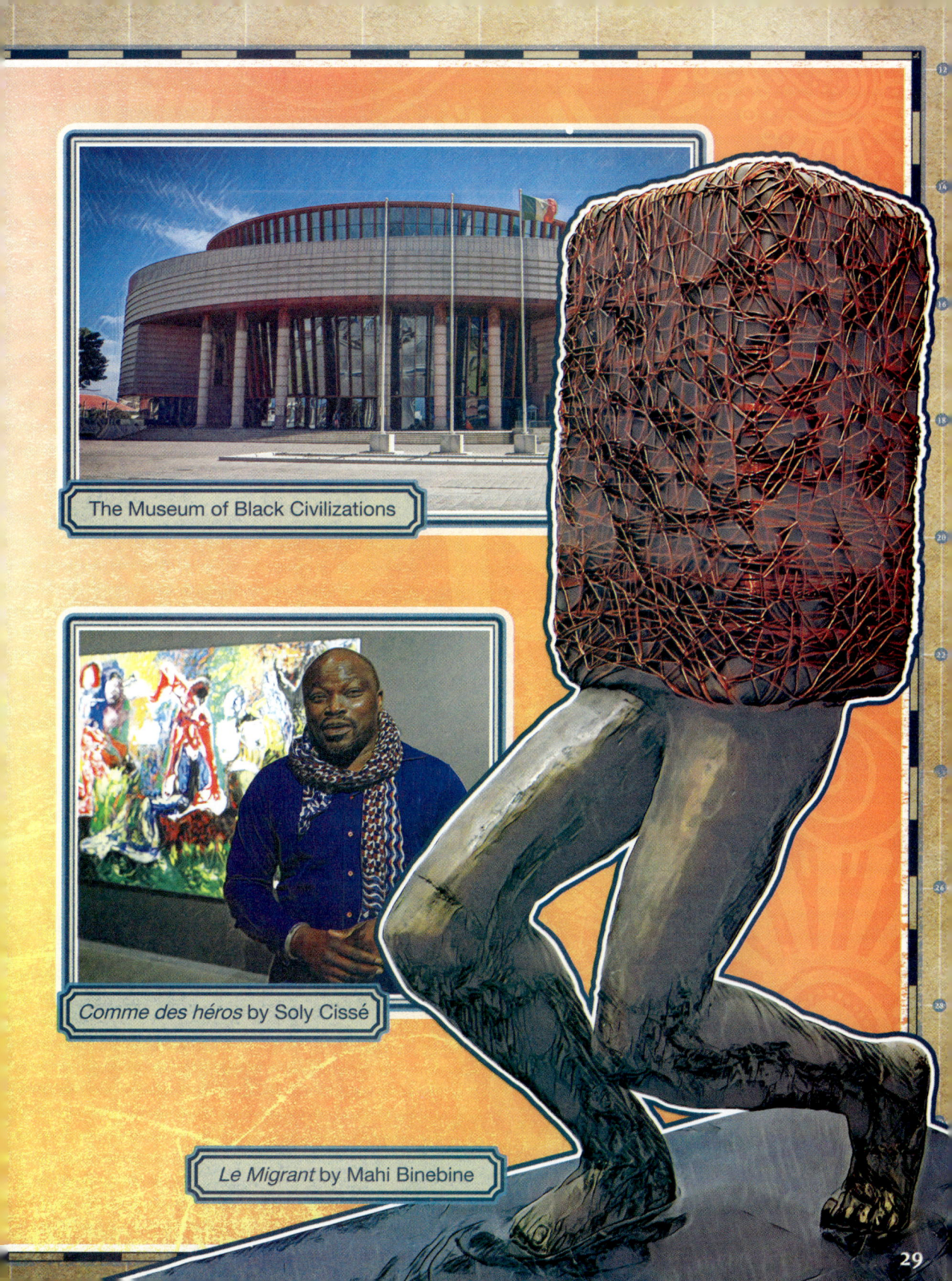

The Museum of Black Civilizations

Comme des héros by Soly Cissé

Le Migrant by Mahi Binebine

CREEPY (AND CRAWLY!) COLLECTIONS

Don't look down. Don't look up, either! In fact, you better keep your eyes shut tight. These museum collections are full of ghastly, gruesome, and totally terrifying things. From body parts and insects to funeral objects and haunted prison cells, some museums are very comfortable with the subjects that make us the most *un*comfortable. By exposing visitors to disturbing objects and themes, these collections can help us get used to thinking and talking about life's most difficult subjects. So go ahead, take a look… if you dare!

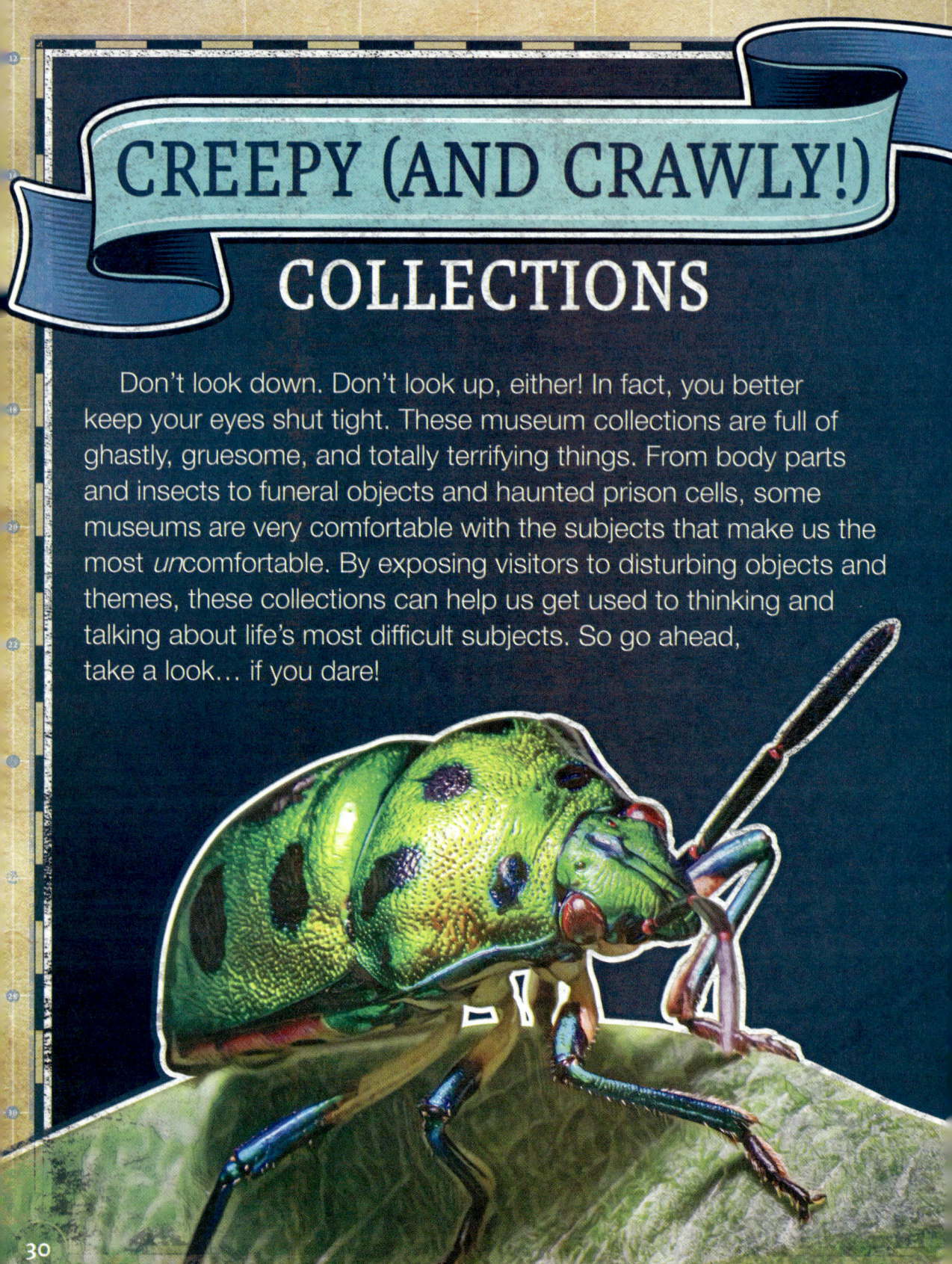

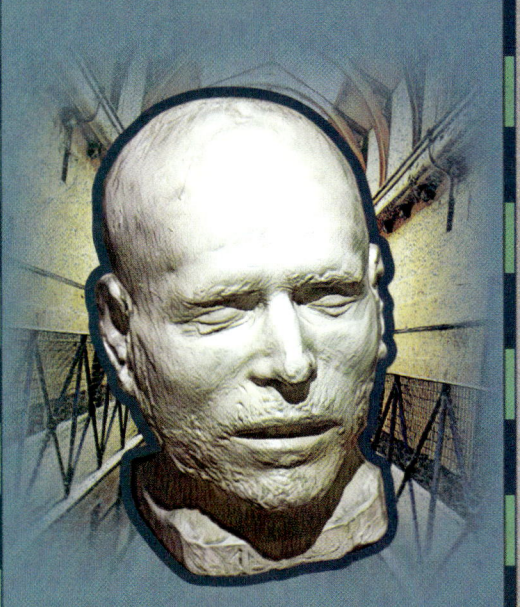

FACING THE PAST

The Old Melbourne Gaol is a prison in Melbourne, Victoria, Australia, that was once home to some of the country's most notorious criminals. Dozens of prisoners were executed on the site, which now houses a collection of death masks. The death masks were created after prisoners were dead. Scientists wanted plaster casts made of the prisoners' heads so that they could study the shapes of the prisoners' skulls.

THE MÜTTER MUSEUM
PHILADELPHIA, PENNSYLVANIA

Pieces of Albert Einstein's brain are on display at the Mütter Museum.

There are history museums…and then there are medical history museums. The Mütter Museum in Philadelphia, Pennsylvania, is known for its detailed collections of human body parts. The museum's glass jars are filled with human hearts, brains, and other organs, and over 3,000 skeletal specimens are on display. It is one of only two collections in the world that contain pieces of Albert Einstein's brain.

In both online and in-person exhibits, viewers can see medical artifacts including old instruments, medicines, prosthetic limbs, and items that were once swallowed and extracted from patients' bodies. Visitors can count 139 human skulls in the Hyrtle Skull Collection. Can't stomach the real thing? The collection also includes highly-detailed wax models of eyeballs, fingers, and full bodies.

THE MUSEUM OF THE TERRACOTTA ARMY
XI'AN, CHINA

Many of the world's greatest collections have been compiled over time and from a variety of sources. But this one was discovered all at once, in 1974. Local farmers outside Xi'an, China, found a few terracotta sculptures buried in deep pits. And then they found more. And more. And more!

Qin Shi Huang, the first emperor of China, built himself a vast collection—an army, actually—to protect his tomb. The underground army, which was buried with the first emperor in 210–209 BCE, is made up of thousands of soldiers, horses, and chariots, along with armor and weapons. Since the shocking discovery was made, the archaeological site has been turned into a museum, and this eerie collection of funerary art frequently travels to museums around the world, where it is shown in special exhibitions.

Ancient tools

THE MEGURO PARASITOLOGICAL MUSEUM

TOKYO, JAPAN

Only check out this collection if you don't mind creatures that make you squirm and scream! The Meguro Parasitological Museum in Tokyo, Japan, is famous for its devotion to parasites—organisms that live on human or animal hosts and often spread disease. The collection includes around 300 unique parasites.

The spine-tingling parasite stories of nematodes and trematodes might get under your skin, but watch out for the tapeworm. The Meguro Parasitological Museum is home to the world's longest tapeworm. Clocking in at 29 feet (8.8 meters) long, this tapeworm is sure to make you lose your appetite.

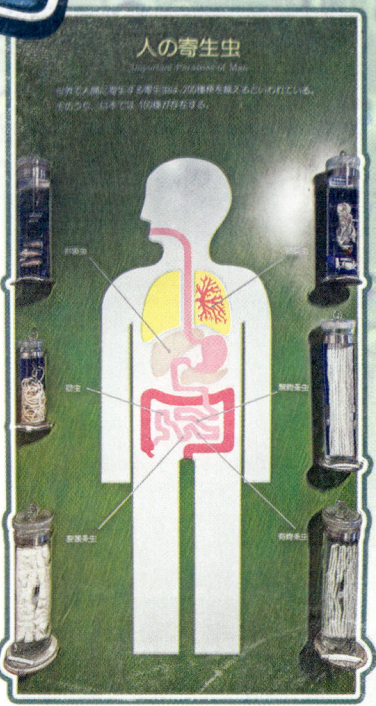

Museum display showing where parasites can be found in the human body

COMMON PARASITIC WORMS

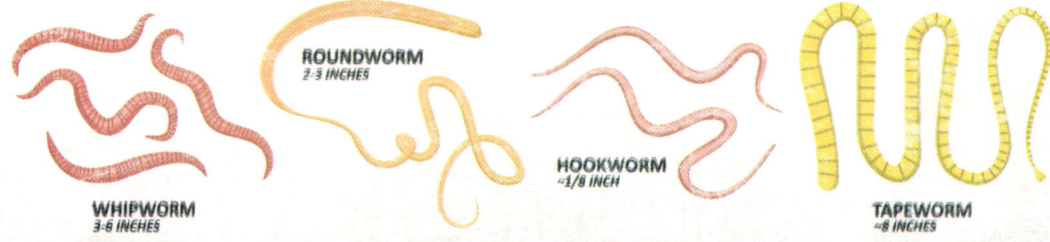

WHIPWORM
3-6 INCHES

ROUNDWORM
2-3 INCHES

HOOKWORM
≈1/8 INCH

TAPEWORM
≈8 INCHES

Tapeworm eggs

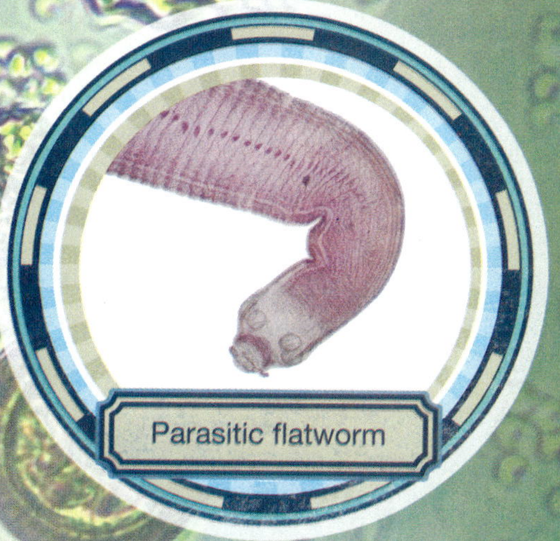

Parasitic flatworm

Female deer tick

BUGGING OUT

What makes this collection of creatures so creepy? It's alive! The O. Orkin Insect Zoo is a permanent exhibit at the Smithsonian Museum of Natural History in Washington, D.C. Since 1976, visitors have been delighted (or disgusted) by tarantulas, butterflies, grasshoppers, worms, and so much more. There's even a 22-million-year-old termite trapped in amber!

INTERACTING WITH ART

Art can touch our hearts. But we aren't usually allowed to touch art! Explore any collection of antiquities or famous artworks, and you'll probably find that you need to stay a few feet away from the objects in order to preserve and protect them. Preservation is important, but some museums are trying something different and asking visitors to interact directly with their exhibits!

THE PLEASE TOUCH MUSEUM
PHILADELPHIA, PENNSYLVANIA

The Please Touch Museum in Philadelphia, Pennsylvania, was designed to be a hands-on, interactive experience for kids. Their collection of engaging exhibits includes a historic carousel, rocket room, imagination playground, and an indoor treehouse. Kids and their families can make and create their way through experiential exhibits. The museum's art studio, makerspace, and theater give guests the chance to become artists, inventors, and actors. They might even see their creations up on the walls of the Please Touch Museum someday.

MUSIC TO MY EARS (AND EYES!)

This collection can be seen, heard, and touched. The Musical Instrument Museum in Phoenix, Arizona, features over 15,000 musical instruments and music-related artifacts from around the world. When instruments aren't on display, they are cleaned, repaired, and restored in the Conservation Lab. In the Experience Gallery, guests are encouraged to play a tune on everything from a Peruvian harp to a West African djembe.

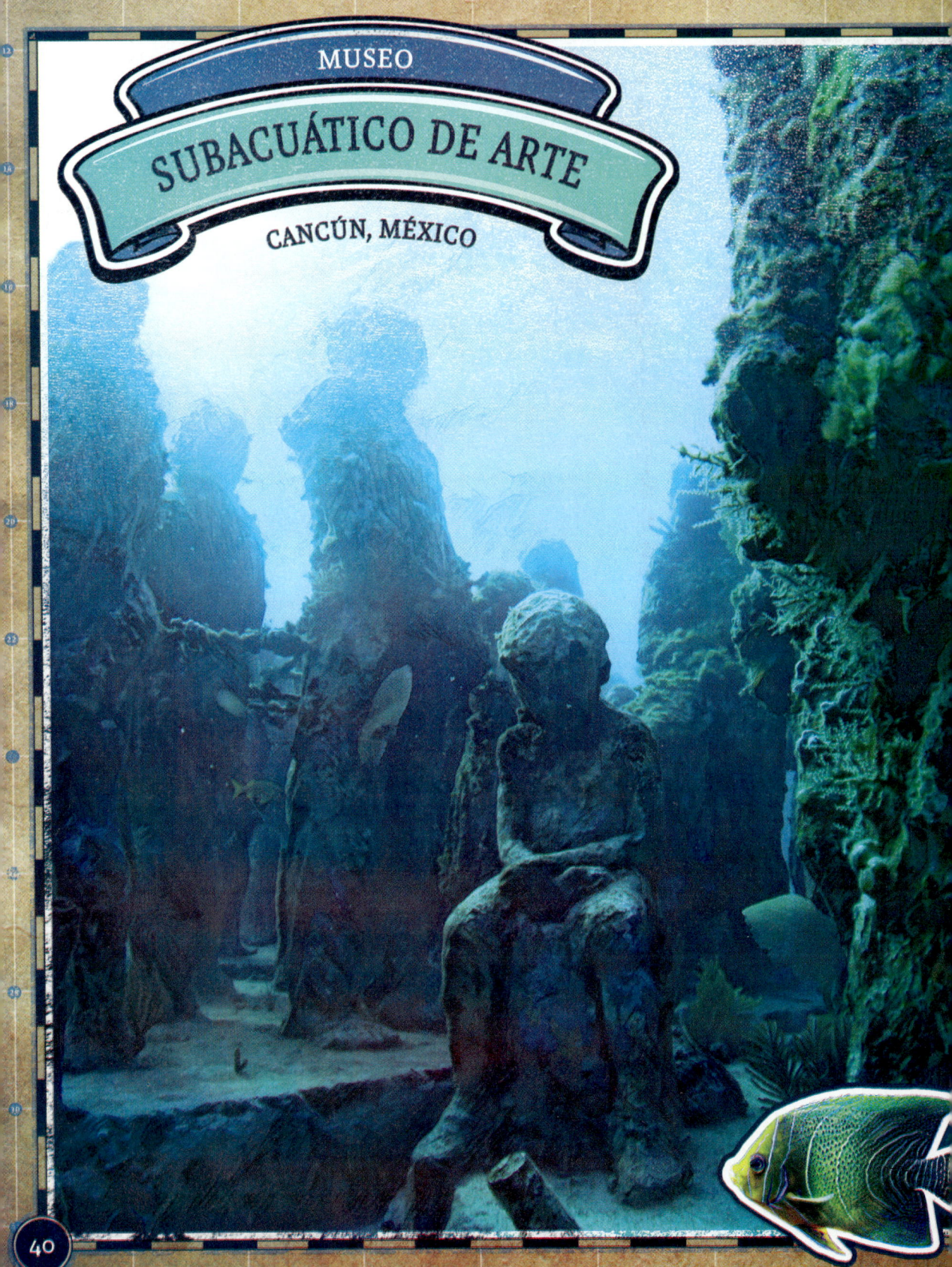

MUSEO SUBACUÁTICO DE ARTE

CANCÚN, MÉXICO

To see this collection, you'll have to get a little wet! *Museo Subacuático de Arte* or Underwater Museum of Art (MUSA) is located in Cancún, México. Visitors suit up and dive under the ocean's surface to see a massive collection of over 500 sculptures.

Built to help conserve and call attention to nearby coral reefs, the museum features human figures, furniture, and even a full-sized car. Each sculpture is made with a special concrete that, when placed underwater, helps to create corals. Keep your eyes open for sea creatures! Sea turtles and colorful fish are frequent museum visitors. For those who don't want to dive deep, a glass-bottomed boat can offer a cool-but-comfortable view of the collection.

A historical interpreter recreating life in a tin shop in rural New England in the 1970s

COLLECTIONS COME ALIVE

At living history museums, historical settings are recreated to give visitors the experience of traveling back in time. Visitors can go inside collections of historically accurate buildings, participate in activities from the period, and even talk with historical interpreters, or actors who seem as though they were plucked from the past.

THE CITY MUSEUM
ST. LOUIS, MISSOURI

The City Museum in St. Louis is taking museum play to the next level. Artist Bob Cassilly created the museum out of an old shoe factory. The building now houses all sorts of oversized artistic creations, including a giant pencil, a massive whale, and the World's Largest Underwear!

At the City Museum, kids and adults are encouraged to climb and play their way through every inch of the collection. Explore the caves and find mythical creatures, run on a hamster wheel, crawl through a web of tunnels, and slip down a ten-story slide. Brave guests who make it to the rooftop can go inside a school bus that dangles off the building and even meet a 24-foot metal praying mantis. New objects are added to this quirky collection every year. Who knows how it will grow in the future?

Inside an airplane cockpit at the museum

The ten-story spiral slide inside the museum

MonstroCity is an interactive sculpture/playground in front of the museum

43

WE TRAVELED TO...

Find the location of each place you've traveled to while reading this book.

1. **The Louvre:** Paris, France
2. **The British Museum:** London, England
3. **The Met:** New York City, New York
4. **The National Mustard Museum:** Middleton, Wisconsin
5. **The Museum of Bread Culture:** Ulm, Germany
6. **The Sulabh International Museum of Toilets:** Delhi, India
7. **The Neon Museum:** Las Vegas, Nevada
8. **The NMAAHC:** Washington, D.C.
9. **Te Papa:** Wellington, New Zealand
10. **The Egyptian Museum:** Cairo, Egypt
11. **The Museum of Black Civilizations:** Dakar, Senegal
12. **The Mütter Museum:** Philadelphia, Pennsylvania
13. **Museum of the Terracotta Army:** Xi'an, China
14. **The Meguro Parasitological Museum:** Tokyo, Japan
15. **The Please Touch Museum:** Philadelphia, Pennsylvania
16. **MUSA:** Cancún, México
17. **The City Museum:** St. Louis, Missouri

GLOSSARY

antiquities (an-TIK-wuh-teez): relics or artifacts of ancient times

artifacts (AHU-tuh-fakts): objects made or changed by humans, especially from the past

bicultural (bai-KUHL-chur-uhl): combining the customs of two nations or cultures

colonized (KAH-luh-nized): settled on and established political control over an area

conserved (kuhn-SURVD): protected from harm or destruction

curator (KYOOR-ay-tur): a person who is in charge of parts of a museum collection

deaccessions (dee-ik-SESH-uhnz): the official removal of an object from a collection

exhibition (ek-suh-BISH-uhn): a public display of work

Indigenous (in-DI-juh-nes): those who are native to a particular place

preservation (prez-ur-VAY-shuhn): keeping something in original or good condition

repatriation (ree-pay-tree-AY-shuhn): the return of someone or something to the country of origin

restored (RI-stord): brought something back to its former condition

INDEX

Africa 10, 28
African 22, 23, 28, 39
Art 4, 7, 8, 10, 11, 22, 28, 34, 38
China 34
Egypt 9, 26, 27
food 12, 14, 15
historical interpreter(s) 41
history 5, 7, 8, 12, 16, 18, 22, 23, 24, 26, 32, 37, 41
Japan 12, 19, 36
Louvre 6, 7
music 39
Smithsonian 22, 37
toilet(s) 12, 18, 19

TEXT-DEPENDENT QUESTIONS

1. What is the world's largest museum?

2. Why are more and more museum collections being digitized?

3. Why do cultural museums exist? Why are they important?

4. How can creepy collections be a good thing?

5. What are some museums with interactive, hands-on collections?

EXTENSION ACTIVITY

It's fun to travel the world, visit museums, and check out collections. But some of the greatest groups of art and other objects can be found right in your own backyard! Go online to see if museums, libraries, or universities near you are currently displaying any collections. Make a plan to go see them! You might discover a collection even cooler than the ones in this book.

BIBLIOGRAPHY

Asma, Stephen T. *Stuffed Animals & Pickled Heads: The Culture and Evolution of Natural History Museums*. Oxford: Oxford University Press, 2001.

El-Geressi, Yasmine. "Egypt Wants Its Treasures Back." Majalla. July 19, 2019. https://eng.majalla.com/node/73996/egypt-wants-its-treasures-back (accessed May 24, 2021).

Felch, Jason. *Chasing Aphrodite: The Hunt for Looted Antiquities at the World's Richest Museum*. Boston: Houghton Mifflin Harcourt, 2011.

Gross, Jenny. "A Jane Austen Museum Wants to Discuss Slavery. Will Her Fans Listen?" New York Times. April 27, 2021. https://www.nytimes.com/2021/04/27/world/europe/jane-austen-slavery-museum.html (accessed May 10, 2021).

Hollein, Max. "Building and Caring for the Met Collection." The Met. February 17, 2021. https://www.metmuseum.org/blogs/now-at-the-met/2021/building-and-caring-for-the-met-collection (accessed May 245, 2021).

Knowles, Hannah. "As plantations talk more honestly about slavery, some visitors are pushing back." Washington Post. September 8, 2019. https://www.washingtonpost.com/history/2019/09/08/plantations-are-talking-more-about-slavery-grappling-with-visitors-who-talk-back/ (accessed May 9, 2021).

Lonetree, Amy. *Decolonizing Museums: Representing Native America in National and Tribal Museums*. Chapel Hill, NC: University of North Carolina Press, 2012.

Louvre. "Explore." Louvre. https://www.louvre.fr/en/explore (accessed May 13, 2021).

Lubar, Steven. Inside the Lost Museum: Curating, Past and Present. Cambridge, MA: Harvard University Press, 2017.

Lubow, Arthur. "Terra Cotta Soldiers on the March." Smithsonian Magazine. July, 2009. https://www.smithsonianmag.com/history/terra-cotta-soldiers-on-the-march-30942673/ (accessed May 24, 2021).

Schuessler, Jennifer. "What Should Museums Do With the Bones of the Enslaved?" New York Times. April 20, 2021. https://www.nytimes.com/2021/04/20/arts/design/museums-bones-smithsonian.html (accessed May 10, 2021).

Small, Zachary. "National Gallery of Art Reopens With a New Vision: 'For All the People.'" New York Times. May 13, 2021. https://www.nytimes.com/2021/05/13/arts/design/national-gallery-washington-reopen-rebrand.html (accessed May 20, 2021).

Smithsonian Institution. "The Smithsonian Institution Fact Sheet." April 7, 2020. Smithsonian Institution. https://www.si.edu/newsdesk/factsheets/smithsonian-institution-fact-sheet (accessed May 18, 2021).

UNESCO. "Museums." UNESCO. https://en.unesco.org/themes/museums (accessed May 12, 2021).

Waxman, Sharon. Loot: The Battle over the Stolen Treasures of the Ancient World. New York: Times Books, 2008.

Kaitlyn Duling collects pins, patches, and an old toy called Polly Pocket! An avid reader and writer who grew up in Illinois, she now resides in Washington, D.C., where she loves to visit the Smithsonian museums. Kaitlyn has written more than 100 books for children and teens.

© 2022 Rourke Educational Media

All rights reserved. No part of this book may be reproduced or utilized in any form or by any means, electronic or mechanical including photocopying, recording, or by any information storage and retrieval system without permission in writing from the publisher.

www.rourkeeducationalmedia.com

PHOTO CREDITS ©: Cover: Andrey_Kuzmin/ Shuterstock.com; Cover: MrsWilkins/ Getty Images; Cover: Petr Bonek/ Shutterstock.com; Cover: ricorico/ Getty Images; Cover: Waeel quttene/ Shutterstock.com; Cover: Danita Delimont Photography/Newscom; Cover: ricorico/ Getty Images; All Pages: Andrey_Kuzmin/ Shutterstock.com; Page 1: ricorico/ Getty Images; Page 1: Primi2 / Shutterstock.com; Page 3: MrsWilkins/ Getty Images; Page 4: M.Uljmanski/ Shutterstock.com; Page 5: Prachaya Roekdeethaweesab/ Shutterstock.com; Page 5: Hung Chung Chih / Shutterstock.com; Page 6: Gao Jing Xinhua News Agency/Newscom, Page 6: Gao Jing Xinhua News Agency/Newscom; Page 6: KrimKate/ Shutterstock.com; Page 6: zefart / Shutterstock.com; Page 6: S-F / Shutterstock.com; Page 7: elena bee / Shutterstock.com; Page 7: Africa Studio/Shutterstock; Page 8: Takashi Images / Shutterstock.com; Page 8: Dan Breckwoldt / Shutterstock.com; Page 9: Andrea Izzotti / Shutterstock.com; Page 9: ZoranMilisavljevic83/ Shutterstock.com; Page 9: Mark Coggins/ Getty Images; Page 10: ELEPHOTOS / Shutterstock.com; Page 10: Pit Stock / Shutterstock.com; Page 10: Targa56 / Shutterstock.com; Page 10: Andrea Izzotti / Shutterstock.com; Page 11: Mark Rademaker/ Shutterstock.com; Page 11: Susanne Pommer/ Shutterstock.com; Page 11: Andy Dean Photography/ Shutterstock.com; Page 12: St Petersburg Times/Tampa Bay Times/ZUMAPRESS.com; Page 12: Hussmann/ Shutterstock.com; Page 12: Bragapictures/ Shutterstock.com; Page 12: Primi2 / Shutterstock.com; Page 13: Afanasiev Andrii/ Shutterstock.com; Page 13: Khosro/ Shutterstock.com; Page 13: Waeel quttene/ Shutterstock.com; Page 13: Aquarius Studio/ Shutterstock.com; Page 13: Africa Studio/ Shutterstock.com; Page 13: Petr Malyshev/ Shutterstock.com; Page 14: Roberto Galan / Shutterstock.com; Page 14: Spalnic/ Shutterstock.com; Page 15: SpicyTruffel / Shutterstock.com; Page 15: aimy27feb/ Shutterstock.com; Page 15: ELAKSHI CREATIVE BUSINESS/ Shutterstock.com; Page 16: Stefan Puchner/dpa/picture-alliance/Newscom; Page 16: Stefan Puchner/dpa/picture-alliance/Newscom; Page 17: Stefan Puchner/dpa/picture-alliance/Newscom; Page 18: Bi Xiaoyang Xinhua News Agency/Newscom; Page 18: Bodor Tivadar/ Shutterstock.com; Page 19: Bi Xiaoyang Xinhua News Agency/Newscom; Page 19: Bi Xiaoyang Xinhua News Agency/Newscom; Page 19: Bi Xiaoyang Xinhua News Agency/Newscom; Page 20: The Neon Museum/ZUMA Wire/ZUMAPRESS.com; Page 20: Danita Delimont Photography/Newscom; Page 20: GagliardiPhotography / Shutterstock.com; Page 21: Nagel Photography / Shutterstock.com; Page 22: Jim Thompson/ZUMAPRESS/Newscom; Page 23: Terri Laurens / Shutterstock.com; Page 23: CNP/AdMedia/SIPA/Newscom; Page 23: DavidNNP / Shutterstock.com; Page 24: Rafael Ben-Ari/ Chameleons Eye/Newscom; Page 25: dpa/Newscom; Page 25: squarelogo/ Shutterstock.com; Page 25: WeinhÃ¤upl/Newscom; Page 26: lexan / Shutterstock.com; Page 27: Claudio Divizia / Shutterstock.com; Page 27: Orhan Cam / Shutterstock.com; Page 27: Galyna Andrushko/ Shutterstock.com; Page 28: ZOHRA BENSEMRA/REUTERS/Newscom; Page 29: ZOHRA BENSEMRA/REUTERS/Newscom; Page 29: ZOHRA BENSEMRA/REUTERS/Newscom; Page 29: Xinhua/Newscom; Page 29: Galiya Zamaletdinova/ Shutterstock.com; Page 30: Picturesque_pixels/ Shutterstock.com; Page 31: FilipTravelWorld / Shutterstock.com; Page 31: David Wall / DanitaDelimont.com "Danita Delimont Photography"/Newscom; Page 31: matiascausa/ Shutterstock.com; Page 32: Guido Kirchner/dpa/picture-alliance/Newscom; Page 33: matiascausa/ Shutterstock.com; Page 34: DnDavis / Shutterstock.com; Page 34: thesixthfloor89 / Shutterstock.com; Page 34: lapas77 / Shutterstock.com; Page 35: Lukas Hlavac / Shutterstock.com; Page 35: Primi2 / Shutterstock.com; Page 36: Christopher Jue/AFLO/Newscom; Page 36: logika600/ Shutterstock.com; Page 36: frank60/ Shutterstock.com; Page 37: Tilegen/ Shutterstock.com; Page 37: Jarun Ontakrai/ Shutterstock.com; Page 37: Choksawatdikorn/ Shutterstock.com; Page 37: KPixMining/ Shutterstock.com; Page 38: Igori_K/ Shutterstock.com; Page 39: Michael Candelori/ZUMA Press/Newscom; Page 39: Alona_S/ Shutterstock.com; Page 39: Billion Photos/ Shutterstock.com; Page 39: John Greim/Newscom; Page 41: Ritu Manoj Jethani / Shutterstock.com; Page 41: Krofoto/ Shutterstock.com; Page 41: COLORART_DESIGN_STUDIO/ Shutterstock.com; Page 42: Joshua Janes / Keep Turning, LLC; Page 42: Joshua Janes / Keep Turning, LLC; Page 43: Joshua Janes / Keep Turning, LLC; Page 43: Joshua Janes / Keep Turning, LLC; Page 43: Joshua Janes / Keep Turning, LLC; Page 44: Juliann/ Shutterstock.com

Library of Congress PCN Data

Coolest Collections / Kaitlyn Duling
(Travel to...)
ISBN 978-1-73165-183-9 (hard cover)
ISBN 978-1-73165-228-7 (soft cover)
ISBN 978-1-73165-198-3 (e-Book)
ISBN 978-1-73165-213-3 (e-Pub)
Library of Congress Control Number: 2021944518

Rourke Educational Media
Printed in the United States of America
05-1452413123

Edited by: **Hailey Scragg**
Cover and interior design by: **Joshua Janes**